Simply Science

LAND TRANSPORTATION

Discover Science Through Facts and Fun

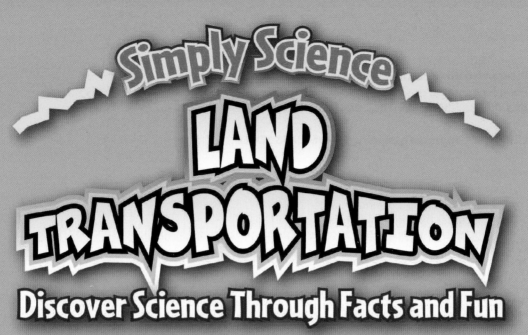

By Steve Way and Gerry Bailey

Science and curriculum consultant:
Debra Voege, M.A., science curriculum resource teacher

Gareth Stevens
Publishing

Please visit our web site at www.garethstevens.com.
For a free catalog describing our list of high-quality books, call 1-800-542-2595 (USA)
or 1-800-387-3178 (Canada). Our fax: 1-877-542-2596

Library of Congress Cataloging-in-Publication Data

Way, Steve.
    Land Transportation/by Steve Way.
      p. cm.—(Simply Science)
      Includes bibliographical references and index.
      ISBN-10: 0-8368-9228-3   ISBN-13: 978-0-8368-9228-4 (lib. bdg.)
      1. Transportation—Juvenile literature. I. Title.
    TA1149.W39   2009
    629.04'9—dc22   2008012421

This North American edition first published in 2009 by
Gareth Stevens Publishing
A Weekly Reader® Company
1 Reader's Digest Road
Pleasantville, NY 10570-7000 USA

This edition copyright © 2009 by Gareth Stevens, Inc. Original edition copyright © 2007 by
Diverta Publishing Ltd., First published in Great Britain by Diverta Publishing Ltd., London, UK.

Gareth Stevens Senior Managing Editor: Lisa M. Herrington
Gareth Stevens Creative Director: Lisa Donovan
Gareth Stevens Designer: Keith Plechaty
Gareth Stevens Associate Editor: Amanda Hudson
Special thanks to Mark Sachner

Photo Credits: Cover (tc) NASA/JPL/Cornell University, (bl) Mike Butler/Shutterstock Inc.; p. 5
PCL/Alamy; p. 9 Dorling Kindersley Images; p. 12 Dorling Kindersley Images; p. 16 Piotr
Przeszlo/Shutterstock Inc.; p. 19 Sean Sexton/Corbis; p. 21 Mike Butler/Shutterstock Inc.; p. 23 Dorling
Kindersley courtesy of the National Motor Museum, Beaulieu; p. 24 (t) Daimler Chrysler AG; (b) The Car
Photo Library; p. 25 (t) Christophe Testi/Shutterstock Inc. (m) Andres Rodriguez/Shutterstock Inc. (b)
The Motoring Picture Library.; p. 27 Jolin/Shutterstock Inc.; p. 28 NASA/Johnson Space Center; p. 29
NASA/JPL/Cornell University.

Illustrations: Steve Boulter and Xact Studio

Diagrams: Ralph Pitchford

Printed in the United States of America

1 2 3 4 5 6 7 8 9 10 09 08

CONTENTS

Faster and Easier!

Ever since prehistoric times, people have needed to travel from place to place. As time went on, they needed to go faster. They also needed to carry more goods with them. The invention of the wheel made life easier for ancient people.

But our ancient ancestors could never have imagined the different land **vehicles** we would create in the centuries that followed.

As you will find out from this book, land vehicles:

take us across different kinds of land around the world,

carry our loads,

help us work, and

even explore other worlds!

Slipping and Sliding

If you've ever been in a car that slipped and slid on snowy roads, you know that wheels often don't work very well on snow. People have come up with other ways to travel in slippery conditions!

Sleighs and Sleds

Sleighs and sleds use runners for sliding instead of wheels. Even though the sleigh is an ancient invention, it's still one of the best vehicles to use in thick snow! Many polar explorers used sleighs to pull their loads.

On sleds and sleighs, **runners** glide easily over smooth surfaces such as snow or ice.

Skis

Skis were originally used by people living in snowy places who needed to travel over soft, powdery snow or ice. Today, skiing is a popular sport all over the world.

Snowmobiles

Snowmobiles are a modern way to travel on snow. They are usually moved by one or two rubber belts that push against the snow. They are steered by skis at the front of the vehicle.

Snowmobiles are often used by reindeer herders instead of sleighs. Sleighs aren't nearly as fast or easy to turn as snowmobiles.

At first, skis were just flat boards. Later, they curved upward at the front to keep them from digging into the snow. The tips of many modern skis also curve inward, toward the middle. This makes the skis easier to turn. Some are even curved upward at the back as well as the front. This allows skiers to go backward and do all sorts of daring stunts!

The Wheel

A wheel is a round disc that can be rolled across the ground. It can then be used to move a load that is placed on top of it.

Wheels help move heavy weights. Many people believe that the wheel was the most important invention ever made. Wheels made travel much easier.

It all looks so simple – now!

Wheels That Help Move Loads

1. Long ago, if you wanted to move a person or a heavy load, you had to drag or push the load along the ground.

2. This meant using muscle power!

Friction

When moving objects touch, they rub against each other. We call this rubbing movement **friction**. Friction causes moving objects to slow down. We see the effects of friction all around us. When you fall and your elbow gets scraped, it is because of friction between your elbow and the floor.

These children are using friction to rub things smooth.

3. The idea for a wheel probably came to someone who used rolling logs to help move a load. Think of how hard it must have been to have to move the logs from the back to the front as the load moved forward.

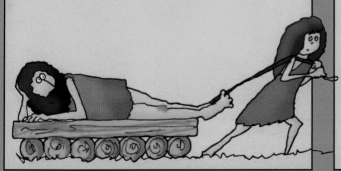

4. The biggest problem would have been a rubbing force we call friction. However hard the load was pushed and pulled, friction would have worked against the forward movement.

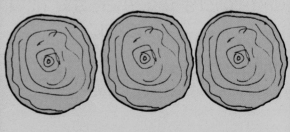

How the Wheel Developed

No one knows who invented the wheel. Some people think it was in use as early as 8,000 years ago. The oldest wheel known is 5,500 years old. It was found in a part of Asia known as **Sumeria**.

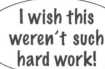

I wish this weren't such hard work!

Runners and Rollers

1. Long ago, people put rollers under heavy objects so they could be moved more easily. The rollers had to be carried from the back to the front as the load moved forward.

2. Runners were invented to help move loads. Runners are like sleds. Using runners and rollers together, the load could be more easily dragged along.

Horsepower

The speed at which a vehicle moves is often measured in horsepower. One horsepower is equal to the power needed to lift 1 pound (.5 kilogram) 33,000 feet (10,058 meters) in one minute.

3. In time, the runners wore **grooves** into the rollers. People then cut away the wood between the grooves. This made an **axle** joined to a wheel at each end.

4. The wheels were cut off the axle, and a hole was cut through the middle of each wheel. Then the wheel could spin on the axle. Spinning wheels moved things even faster.

The Chariot

A chariot is a fast kind of cart. Carts were simple vehicles used to carry loads. They had two or four wheels and were usually pulled along by cattle or horses. But chariots had just two spoked wheels. They were light and easy to steer and mainly used in battle.

Spoked Wheels

The wheel was improved by the Egyptians. They made wheels with more than two spokes for their chariots. Slimmer spokes made the wheels lighter.

Wheels With Spokes

1. The first carts were heavy wooden vehicles. They were used by farmers to haul hay, vegetables, and other heavy loads. But they weren't good for carrying soldiers into battle. Strong armies needed something faster.

2. They needed something light and springy that would travel fast and turn corners easily.

3. The old carts needed some changes! The first things that were changed were the wheels. The old cart wheels were solid and heavy. The wheels needed to be lighter.

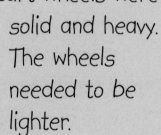

4. So people tried cutting sections out of the solid wheel centers.

5. People kept cutting away wood until only light spokes joined the wheel to the **hub** in the middle. The wheels were lighter and faster, and they bounced more smoothly over bumps.

Other Road Vehicles

Modern cars have only been around for a short while. Other kinds of vehicles have been on the roads for thousands of years.

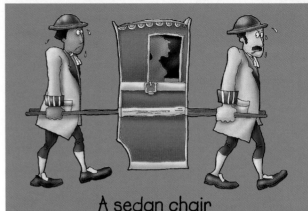

A sedan chair

2. In the 17th century, the sedan chair was developed in Sedan, a town in France. The passenger sat on an enclosed chair. Two people used handles to carry it.

Later came the rickshaw—a type of chair pulled along on wheels.

1. The Romans built a lot of roads. The roads were used by people on foot. But they were also used by carts and wagons that were pulled by animals.

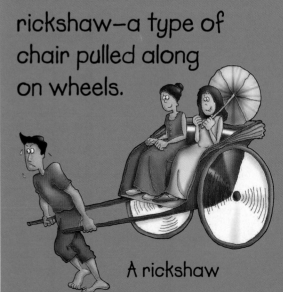

A rickshaw

3. As time went on, larger coaches were developed and used to move people around towns. Stagecoaches were used for traveling around the country from town to town.

A horse-drawn bus

4. From 1834 until cars became popular, carriages known as hansom cabs were used in cities. These carriages had two large wheels and could carry two people.

A hansom cab

5. Early in the 19th century, horse-drawn carriages were used in Paris, France, to carry people around the city. Later in the same century, steam-driven buses were used.

A stagecoach

Tires

When cars were invented, wheels had to change. Car makers put a band of rubber or rubber-like material around the rim of each wheel. This is called a tire.

The tread is a pattern cut into the rubber tire. The tread helps tires grip the road.

A Smooth Ride

1. Early cars were uncomfortable to ride in. The first cars had wheels more like wagon wheels than tires. They were hard to control.

2. The car makers started using **pneumatic** tires. These are rubber tires with inner tubes filled with air. Over time, the tires were improved.

3. Tires with grooves cut into the rubber, called treads, gave the car a better grip on the road.

Wire Tires

Special tires were used on the lunar roving vehicle that explored the Moon. Instead of being pumped with air, the rover's tires were made of a special lightweight metal made out of woven piano wire!

4. Spare tires were added to cars so drivers could get going again if the tire popped.

5. It wasn't until World War II (1939-1945) that strong, wide tires without inner tubes were developed. These tires made an air-tight seal with the wheel hub.

6. Radial tires are put on modern cars. They are made with layers of strong wire cords running **diagonally** around the inside of the tire. They are safe at high speeds. They have a good grip.

Bicycle

A bike, or bicycle, is a vehicle that has two wheels. It is powered by the rider. One wheel is behind the other. Both wheels are held in place by a frame.

Early Models

The first pedal bike was called a velocipede, or "boneshaker." It had no springs and was a bumpy ride. The penny-farthing came later. It had one huge wheel at the front and a tiny one at the rear.

Finally the "safety bicycle" was invented. It had two wheels of equal size and was much easier to ride. This is the kind of bike we ride today.

Penny-farthing bike

The Bike

1. Not long ago, most people had to get around by walking. So they usually didn't travel too far from home!

2. Wealthier people could ride a horse or take a stagecoach. For most people, walking was the only cheap and easy way to travel.

3. Surely there had to be a way to carry a person along on wheels. People were strong enough to push wheels around. But could they use wheels to carry themselves quickly across the ground?

4. At last, the bicycle was invented. Two wheels were joined together by an axle and attached to a frame. Pedals were attached to the axle. As the rider's feet turned the pedals, the wheels turned, too. The rider could sit above the wheels and steer with handlebars.

The Steam Locomotive

A steam locomotive is a vehicle that is powered by a steam engine. It is used to pull railroad cars or trucks along iron rails.

Steam Engine

Coal is burned in the furnace to heat water in the boiler and make steam. The steam pushes a piston, which drives the wheels.

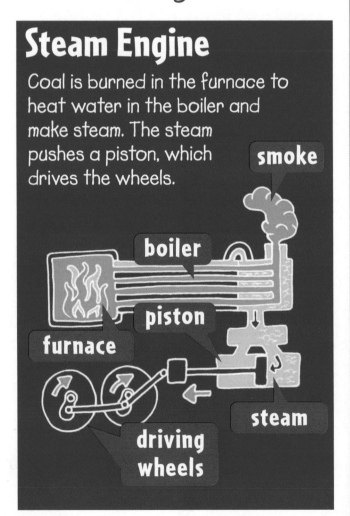

- smoke
- boiler
- piston
- furnace
- steam
- driving wheels

Steam That Turns Wheels

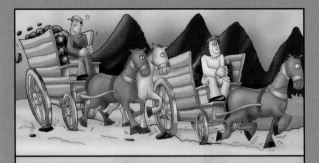

1. Up to the 1800s, many factory owners had to use a horse-drawn cart to carry their goods from place to place.

2. Then an inventor named Richard Trevithick had an idea to build a pulling machine.

3. Trevithick invented a steam-powered engine. Steam from the steam engine pushes against a **piston** in a **cylinder** at the side of the locomotive. The piston then pushes the big driving wheels.

I'll burn coal to heat water and make steam.

4. As the piston moves backward and forward in the cylinder, it turns the wheels.

Railroads

Steam locomotives ran on iron rails. This made the ride smooth and fast. Soon a network of powerful steam locomotives crisscrossed every major country of the world. Railroads carried goods and people. They also connected cities.

This is an old steam locomotive from the American West. The railroads led to the movement of goods and people across the country in the 1800s.

The Automobile

An automobile is a road vehicle that is usually powered by a motor known as the internal combustion engine.

Hello. I'm Karl Benz – the man who invented the first true gasoline automobile.

Internal Combustion Engine

Inside an internal combustion engine, a moving piston draws in air and helps squeeze the air. The squeezed air gets very hot. A jet of gasoline is mixed with the hot air and explodes. This sudden power pushes the piston down, which turns a crankshaft. This happens over and over again very fast, driving the car forward.

exploding fuel mixture

piston

crankshaft

1. A German inventor named Karl Benz was interested in developing the automobile as a new form of transportation. He built an internal combustion engine that could be used in an everyday carriage. He placed the engine in the back and attached it to the rear wheels.

Benz's Car

Benz built his little three-wheeled car in 1885 and sold his first one two years later. He built a four-wheeled model in 1893.

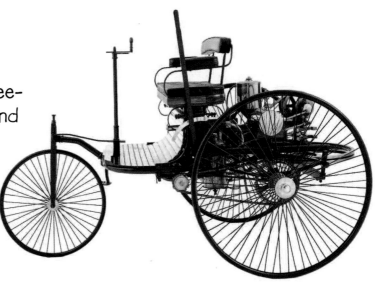

2. The engine had pistons inside cylinders. When gasoline and air were ignited by a spark, the pistons pushed down and turned a crankshaft. The shaft was attached to the two back wheels by a chain.

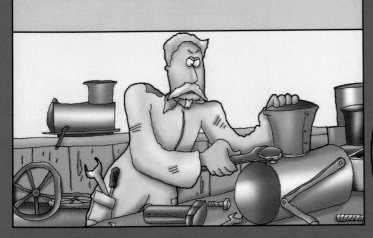

3. The front wheel was fitted with a handle. That's how the car was steered.

Cars

The design of cars has changed since Karl Benz made his three-wheeled car. Early car makers like Benz and Gottlieb Daimler based their designs on vehicles they were familiar with—horse-drawn carriages. Their cars were sometimes called "horseless carriages."

Early car designs were sometimes called three-box designs. They had a "box" for the engine, one to carry the passengers, and one for the luggage. Unfortunately, boxes are not the sort of shape that moves easily through the air. They're not streamlined.

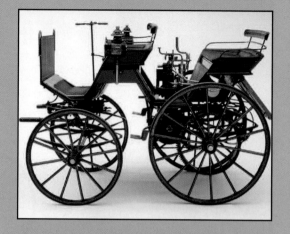

The Daimler car was adapted from a horse-drawn carriage.

Enclosed Cars

Early cars were open-topped and uncomfortable to ride in. So makers began designing cars with the engine at the front and a closed body behind to keep passengers warm and dry.

Mass Production

Henry Ford developed a way of making hundreds of cars at a time by putting them together piece by piece on an assembly line in a huge factory. The parts were all a standard size, so cars all looked the same. But they became much cheaper. More and more people could afford to buy them.

Aerodynamics

Designers knew they had to make their cars more streamlined, or **aerodynamic**, so they would move faster. They shaved off the square edges and made cars slimmer, more rounded, and sportier.

Hybrids

The less aerodynamic a car is, the more fuel it needs to go quickly. And the more fuel it uses, the more it pollutes the air. Hybrid cars use a mix of gasoline and electricity for power. They are also shaped to move easily through the air and use even less polluting fuel.

Working Vehicles

Tractors are machines needed to plow land and haul crops and machinery from place to place. These strong farm machines need to travel on rough and muddy land without getting stuck. They need special tires.

The Plow

Before tractors, animal-drawn plows were used to turn the soil for thousands of years.

Steam Tractor

The first tractor powered by steam arrived in the 1770s. The engine and boiler were placed above the front wheel. The tractor was steered using a hand lever. It could move an incredible 8 tons (7,257 kg). But it moved at a snail-like speed of just 7.5 miles (12 km) an hour!

A New Track

In the 1900s, an American tractor company developed a kind of wheel known as a caterpillar track. This invention helped heavy tractors move on soft ground without sinking. These were the same caterpillar tracks that were later used on heavy army tanks.

Today's Tractors

Modern tractors must be able to move easily over muddy soil without sinking or slipping. They have front and back wheels that are close together, and the rear wheels are very large. This keeps the tractor firmly on the ground.

I wish we had one of those in my day!

Space Rovers

Land vehicles have even been put to work in space. The space buggy allowed astronauts to travel along the Moon's surface, exploring farther and more safely than they could have done on foot.

Two **solar-powered** rovers, *Opportunity* and *Spirit*, have traveled even farther on Mars than we expected. They have helped us learn more about Mars, our nearest neighboring planet. It's likely that more rovers will be sent to Mars in the near future.

Lunar Rover
Lunar Roving Vehicles were designed to make journeys over the surface of the Moon.

Mars Exploration Rover

NASA's rover called *Spirit* has been exploring the surface of Mars since January 2004 and sending back pictures for scientists to study.

It's pretty bumpy on Mars!

Land Transportation Quiz

1. What do we call the "rubbing" force that slows things down?

2. Where was the oldest known wheel discovered?

3. What is a rickshaw?

4. What was missing from a velocipede, which led to it being called a "boneshaker"?

5. Which inventor came up with the idea for a steam engine that pulled carts?

6. Who had the idea of putting spokes on wheels to make them lighter?

7. Where was the sedan chair first produced?

8. What were the lightweight metal tires of the lunar roving vehicle made from?

9. Who built the first internal combustion engine?

10. Who developed the mass production of cars?

1. Friction 2. Sumeria, Asia 3. A kind of chair pulled on wheels 4. Springs! 5. Richard Trevithick 6. The Egyptians 7. Sedan, France 8. Piano Wire 9. Karl Benz 10. Henry Ford

Glossary

aerodynamic: designed with rounded edges in order to move faster and use less fuel

axle: a pole or bar on which a wheel turns

cylinder: a chamber or hollow tube in which a piston pumps

diagonally: in a slanted direction

friction: the force that slows down objects when they rub against each other

grooves: long, narrow tracks worn or cut into the surface of wood, rubber, or some other material

hub: the central part of a circular object, such as a wheel or a propeller

piston: a solid object that fits tightly within a cylinder. The pumping motion of a piston helps drive a vehicle run by a steam engine or an internal combustion engine.

pneumatic: made to contain or operate with air

runners: narrow surfaces, such as blades or thin strips of wood, on which another object moves

solar-powered: getting power or energy from the light and heat of the Sun

Sumeria: a land in ancient Mesopotamia, which is now part of modern-day Iraq, in western Asia

vehicles: carts, trucks, automobiles, or other objects that are used for transporting people or goods

Index